P9-DSY-870

CAMPING WITH
HENRY AND TOM

Camping
With
Henry and Tom

A NEW PLAY BY

Mark St. Germain

GARDEN CITY, NEW YORK

Copyright © 1995 by Mark St. Germain

CAUTION: Professionals and amateurs are hereby warned that CAMP-
ING WITH HENRY AND TOM is subject to a royalty. It is fully
protected under the copyright laws of the United States of America, and
of all countries covered by the International Copyright Union (including the Dominion of Canada and the rest of the British Common-
wealth), and of all countries covered by the Pan-American Copyright
Convention and the Universal Copyright Convention, and of all countries with which the United States has reciprocal copyright relations.
All rights, including professional, amateur, motion picture, recitation,
lecturing, public reading, radio broadcasting, television, video or sound
taping, all other forms of mechanical or electronic reproduction, such as
information storage and retrieval systems and photocopying, and the
rights of translation into foreign languages, are strictly reserved. Partic-
ular emphasis is laid upon the question of readings, permission for
which must be secured from the author's agent in writing.

The stage performance rights in CAMPING WITH HENRY AND
TOM (other than first class rights) are controlled exclusively by Samuel
French, Inc., 45 West 25th Street, New York, NY 10010. No professional or non-professional performance of the play (excluding first class
professional performance) may be given without obtaining in advance
the written permission of Samuel French, Inc., and paying the requisite
fee.

Inquiries concerning all other rights should be addressed to Mitch
Douglas, c/o International Creative Management, Inc.; 40 West 57th
Street, New York, New York 10019.

Without limiting the rights under copyright reserved above, no part of
this publication may be reproduced, stored in or introduced into a
retrieval system, or transmitted, in any form, or by any means (electronic, mechanical, photocopying, recording, or otherwise), without the
prior written permission of both the copyright owner and the above
publisher of this book.

"Alexander's Ragtime Band" music and lyrics by Irving Berlin
Used by special arrangement with The Rodgers and Hammerstein Or-
ganization on behalf of Irving Berlin Music Company, 1633 Broadway,
Suite 3801, New York, New York 10019.

Photos of the 1995 Off Broadway production at the Lucille Lortel Theatre by Joan Marcus

Design by Maria Chiarino

Manufactured in the U.S.A.

ISBN: 1-56865-148-1

CAMPING WITH HENRY AND TOM was origi-
nally produced at The Berkshire Theatre Festival,
Season 1993: Julianne Boyd, Artistic Director and
Chuck Stills, Managing Director. It opened Off
Broadway at the Lucille Lortel Theatre on February
20, 1995. It was produced by Daryl Roth, Wind
Dancer Theatre, Inc. and Randall L. Wreghitt in
association with Lucille Lortel. It was directed by
Paul Lazarus. The scenery was by James Leonard
Joy; the costumes by Ann Hould-Ward; the lighting
by Phil Monat and sound by Otts Munderloh. Spe-
cial effects were by Gregory Meeh and Leah Kreut-
zer acted as dance consultant. The Production Stage
Manager was Renee Lutz. The cast was as follows:

Henry Ford . . . .   John Cunningham
Warren G. Harding . . . .   Ken Howard
Thomas Alva Edison . . . .   Robert Prosky
Colonel Edmund Starling . . . . . .   John Prosky

THE CAST

HENRY FORD, Industrialist; age fifty-eight

WARREN G. HARDING, Twenty-ninth president of the United States; age fifty-six

THOMAS ALVA EDISON, Inventor; seventy-four years old

COLONEL EDMUND STARLING, Secret Service man; age thirty-five

TIME

July 24, 1921

PLACE:

The woods outside Licking Creek, Maryland

AUTHOR'S NOTE

This play is a fiction suggested by facts. That President Harding went camping with Henry Ford and Thomas Edison is fact; their evening "escape" from the media-packed campsite is fictional. Conversations are fictional, but based on events, documented personal philosophies and the political climate of the time. Though many remarks are adapted from the actual words of these three men, there is no proof that such a dialogue took place. What is indisputable is that Warren G. Harding is a man who never wanted to be President, Henry Ford is a man who did, and after many annual expeditions, this was Thomas Edison's last camping trip with Henry Ford.

MARK ST. GERMAIN

Act One

ACT I

A small clearing surrounded by woods. It is early evening and in the twilight we hear the sound of an approaching Model T touring car and a voice shouting above its motor to be heard.

FORD (*offstage*): It's the truth, like it or not, study the history of any criminal and their first crime's the same: cigarette smoking. (*There is a rustling in the upstage bushes as the voice grows louder*) A man comes to me for a job, I grab his hand, pump "how do you do," and check his fingers for nicotine! Yes, sir! Some folks can't wait for a head start on their fire and brimstone! They'd be puffing away if Lucifer himself was handing out matches!

(Abrupt movement in the foliage as an unseen deer bolts through the wooded area from stage right to left and offstage)

EDISON (*offstage*): HENRY!

HARDING (*offstage*): LOOK OUT! (*There is a thud, a squeal of brakes, a series of crashes, then a final resounding crash as lights come up to reveal a tree toppling over as the Model T crashes into it, throwing the men about. Henry Ford is driving; President Warren G. Harding is beside him. Harding collects himself first*) Is anyone hurt? Mr. Edison?

(*Edison sits up in the backseat*)

EDISON: I don't know yet. Except that I'm a damn sight better off than that deer.

HARDING: Mr. Ford?

FORD (*disgusted*): Aw shit.

EDISON (*can't hear*): Say again?

FORD: "Aw shit"!

EDISON: Mr. Ford is fine.

HARDING (*to Edison*): Let me help you down, sir.

FORD: Why didn't the deer keep running? He just stood there gawking at us!

EDISON: Maybe he never saw a car before.

FORD (*climbing down, inspecting car*): Where the hell has he been? I don't believe this! That four legged son-of-a-bitch cracked our block!

HARDING: I'd better take a look at him. (*Harding exits*)

EDISON: Congratulations, Henry. You are the first man in history to try assassinating a president with wildlife.

FORD: I tried to turn! The deer could have moved, couldn't he, or jumped into the bushes? I think the damn animal was suicidal!

(*Harding enters*)

HARDING: He's still alive. He's stretched out in the dirt, gasping for breath. It's horrible. He keeps staring up at me with those big wet eyes.

EDISON: Looking for Henry, probably.

HARDING: I don't know what we can do. Maybe one of you should take a look at him.

(*Edison and Harding look to Ford*)

FORD: Aw shit. (*Exits*)

HARDING: Look at me, I'm still shaking. Such a beautiful animal. How hunters ever shoot such a magnificent beast for sport is beyond me.

EDISON: A kind of jealousy, I suspect. Or irresistible odds.

HARDING: "Odds"?

EDISON: That the animal won't shoot back.

HARDING: I admire your calm, sir.

EDISON: It's not calm, it's contemplation. I'm appreciating the fact the deer isn't staring at *us* in the road.

(*Ford returns*)

FORD: I don't know why he's not dead! We hit him hard enough to kill my car!

HARDING: Maybe we should put him out of his misery.

FORD: With what? I don't have a gun, do you?

HARDING: No. But we've got to do something!

EDISON: Push the car out for another run at him?

HARDING: Excuse me. (*Harding rushes off*)

FORD: Where's he going?

EDISON: To regurgitate, I expect.

FORD (*shouting after Harding*): Don't worry about the deer! He's coughing blood! He won't last long!

EDISON: You're a comfort, Henry.

FORD: Don't blame this on me! I wasn't driving five miles an hour.

EDISON (*settling down on a log*): Your mouth was doing twice that.

FORD: Somebody had to make conversation! Not all of us can pretend we're stone deaf rather than make small talk. You can't ignore him all weekend! He's the President, for God's sake!

EDISON: I didn't vote for him. I didn't invite him. And I won't call him "Mr. President."

FORD: Call him anything! But at least try to be sociable.

EDISON: How can I outdo you crashing him into a tree? Beat him awhile with a stick, maybe? I'm seventy-four years old; I don't have much "sociability" left.

FORD: All I'm asking is, go easy on him.

EDISON (*hand to ear*): Say again?

FORD (*serious*): Go easy on him. For my sake. (*Edison brushes him off*) I'm asking you as a personal favor.

EDISON (*studying him*): What are you after, Henry?

FORD: Don't you worry.

EDISON: I'm not. He should be.

(*Harding returns*)

HARDING: Colonel Starling has a gun. (*Ford and Edison stare at him*) My Secret Service man. As soon as he gets here, he can put the poor brute out of his misery.

EDISON: Be interesting to see who he shoots.

HARDING (*confused*): The deer. (*Realizes*) Oh, I see, you were making a joke!

EDISON: That's alright. Most of my inventions don't work either.

HARDING: I'm surprised the Colonel hasn't caught up to us already. I know he spotted us; I saw him jump into his car as we were pulling out of camp. He can't be too far back.

FORD (*awkward*): Well, Mr. President, the fact of the matter is that he couldn't have kept up with us.

HARDING: Why's that?

FORD: I pulled out his batt'ry wires.

EDISON (*pause*): I didn't hear that.

HARDING: You did what?

FORD: We wanted to escape, didn't we? Get away from that mob at the campsite, snapping pictures every time we scratch ourselves? I thought we'd get some time to ourselves, put a little adventure into this expedition, that's all.

EDISON: First you try to kill the man, then you kidnap him.

HARDING: Well, if this isn't a hoot! (*He laughs*) Can you imagine them all back there, running in circles, calling the White House! (*Ford tries to laugh with him; Edison does not*) Mr. Ford, I only wish my wife had come along, so I could have left her, too!

FORD: Maybe Mrs. Harding can join us next time.

HARDING: Maybe not. The Duchess isn't one for roughing it.

EDISON: "Roughing it"? We have eight chauffeurs, five maids, seven cooks and a twelve-man crew to pitch our tents. What would luxury be like? Paying people to take our vacations for us?

FORD: But look at us now: surrounded by the genuine article. Real trees, real cold air in our lungs, real dirt under our feet—

EDISON: A real deer in the road.

FORD: An opportunity, that's what it is. An opportunity for all of us to put our feet up and get to know each other.

EDISON: I brought a book . . .

HARDING: Colonel Starling will commandeer another car, don't you think? And once the press boys find out . . .

FORD: There's probably a hundred flash monkeys combing the woods already. And they'll be pretty riled we snuck out from under them.

EDISON: We'll make up for it tomorrow. Spend all day grinning, waving and posing for animal crackers.

FORD: Let's enjoy the wild while we can. What do you say? Nature's laboratory. Birds, bugs and no damned humanity. Look at that stream: cool, beautiful water. If John Burroughs, bless his soul, if John Burroughs was with us this year, he'd talk about that stream for hours: water oblivious to human beings. Glacier fresh, flowing forever. Feeding the creatures of the mountains, then the forests and the marshes, before it pours out to the sea and gets sucked back up in the air to roll down as rain all over again. That's nature for you. That's God on the ball. Just think of it: if I plunked down a hydroelectric plant right over that stream, can you imagine the power I could harness?

HARDING (*pointed*): No, I can't, Mr. Ford. Because we wouldn't want to drag business in to spoil our holi-day, would we? I know I wouldn't. (*Turns away from Ford*) I came to bloviate. Eat, loaf and enjoy this remarkable company. (*Harding takes out a flask*) Gentlemen?

EDISON: No thank you.

FORD: I don't drink. You might as well soak your brain in turpentine.

HARDING: Thanks to Prohibition, the good stuff is hard to find.

EDISON (*opening his book*): You fellows give a holler when we're rescued.

HARDING: I have to hand it to you, Mr. Edison. I never would have had the courage to read all through Bishop Anderson's sermon this afternoon. There we were, sitting like schoolboys trying to look pious enough, and there's Mr. Edison stretched out under a tree with a newspaper.

FORD: I thought it was damn rude and tempting fate on top of that. When it comes to your Judgment Day, Mr. Edison, I hope the Lord takes a break from his Sunday paper.

EDISON: I would have napped, but I'd never get to bed later. Used to sleep two-three hours at night, now I barely do that in a week. When I was younger, I used to like it; it gave me more time to think. The older I get I hate it; it gives me more time to think.

11

There's your divine retaliation, Henry. I'll be dead and no one will know it, I'll still be awake.

HARDING: Until I met the Bishop, I never realized God was so personally concerned with my signing a total abstinence pledge. Do you believe in God, Mr. Edison?

EDISON: A God, yes. It's his middlemen I have no faith in.

(*Sound of bird*)

FORD (*listening*): You hear that?

EDISON: No.

(*Sound of bird*)

FORD: There!

HARDING: The bird?

FORD: Sounds like my wife. That's how we call each other. I come into the house and give Clara one of these—(*Ford does bird call*) And no matter what floor she's on, she'll let fly with one of these—(*does another call*)

EDISON (*not looking up*): We have cats at my house.

(*Harding laughs*)

FORD: Go ahead and poke fun. (*To Edison*) I've seen you with Mrs. Edison, holding hands, tickling at each other's palms. (*To Harding*) They tap Morse code to each other, can you picture that? Two love-sick telegraph operators. It's how he proposed to her.

HARDING: That's charming.

EDISON: It's practical. We can talk behind Henry's back.

FORD: You know what they nicknamed their first two children? "Dot" and "Dash."

EDISON: From what I remember, we had to tap more than fingers to spell them out.

HARDING (*laughing, but a bit too much*): This is swell, isn't it? (*They look at him*) I can see why you men come out here every year; get some time away with the boys. I can't tell you how much I appreciate the invitation, Mr. Ford.

FORD: Henry. Call me Henry.

HARDING: Frankly, "Henry," I don't know if I can get used to calling a genius by his first name.

EDISON (*not looking up*): Call me Mr. Edison. Henry does. It suits me fine.

FORD: Never called him anything else from the first day we met. I was thirty-three years old, just sold my first car for two hundred dollars and there I was at some mechanical convention face to face with my hero. Do you remember that, Mr. Edison?

EDISON (*turning a page*): I trust your memory, Henry.

FORD: I spit ideas at him, couldn't stop myself, and he said, "Son, that's the ticket! The self-contained unit carrying its own fuel! Keep at it!" That kept me going, don't you know.

HARDING: I would say so.

FORD: From then on, Mr. President, whenever I want anything, that's what I do. Keep at it, and keep at it some more. And I don't stop until I get it.

HARDING (*pause*): I have to say when I got your letter, the prospect of spending time with two such famous men was more than a little intimidating.

FORD: How can you say such a thing? You're the President of the United States.

(*Edison looks over his book at Ford, raising his eyebrows; Ford shrugs*)

14

HARDING: That's the voters doing, not mine. But the man who gave us the automobile; who put this country on four tires? We've got more cars than streets; we can't build roads fast enough, ocean to ocean. (*To Edison*) And you, sir; the man who gave us the light bulb, the phonograph! Mr. Edison, when I was a boy, you were no less a hero to me than Caesar or Napoleon.

EDISON: Dead heroes are always the safer choice.

(*Harding laughs; Edison goes back to his book*)

HARDING: Henry, you'll appreciate this. Last week I slipped out of the White House to go down to the Gaiety Burlesque. They put together a special box for me there: All covered up with a hole I can peek through without anyone seeing me. Well, they had a special feature that night, a Charlie Chaplin. "The Kid," have you seen it?

FORD (*seeing Edison's reaction*): No. No . . .

HARDING: You've got to. If you can get in. People line up twice around the block every time they show a new feature. It must make you proud, Mr. Edison, to have given the world such a pleasure as moving pictures.

EDISON (*snapping book shut*): I don't want talk about moving pictures!

15

FORD: Mr. Edison has had his legal problems over the years—

HARDING (*trying to back off*): I'm sorry to hear it—

EDISON: I don't want to talk about lawsuits, either; they're the suicide of time. And I won't discuss patents, judges or the Great American Fairy Tale of justice.

HARDING: Then we won't. All I meant was, when you consider how much good you've done—

EDISON: I'm not a philanthropist, I'm an inventor. I measure success by the size of the silver dollar. Because the last time I checked, "Goodness" wasn't bankable. Now if you'll excuse me, I have a bladder to empty. (*Edison exits behind trees*)

HARDING (*pause*): I seem to have stepped on the lion's tail.

FORD: I don't understand it myself. A man who's accomplished so much. You could fill a museum with all he's created and, between you and me, someday—

(*Edison yells out from the bushes*)

EDISON: I DON'T WANT A DAMN MUSEUM!

HARDING: How could he hear that?

FORD: He's got tricky ears.

(*Edison storms out, fastening his pants*)

EDISON: You know when I invented moving pictures? Thirty years ago! And since then all I've done is re-invent everything I already invented while the whole world sticks its hands in my pockets and robs me blind! I don't need your damn museum, Henry, I'm already a museum! Now change the subject so I can finish pissing in there!

(*Edison goes back into the woods; Ford and Harding move across the clearing*)

HARDING (*pause*): Do you golf?

FORD: Can't say I do. Something about chasing after a little white ball. I tried it once. Felt like a dog throwing my own stick. By the time I got to the third flag, I just grabbed the ball and threw it right down into the hole.

HARDING: I see.

FORD: My son, Edsel, he likes to golf alright. Heading out with his hobnobbers, trailing from Hole 1 to 2 to 3 with everybody else. That's Edsel.

HARDING: It must be wonderful to have your own son working with you. And to take along on trips like this—

FORD: Not much of a choice. I can't leave him at the plant by himself.

HARDING (*pause*): Isn't he running the company?

FORD: The thing is, if I don't keep my eyes on things there'd be no company to run. Last time I went on vacation and left 'em to themselves, I came back and found a whole new car waiting for me. New design, brand new color: Red. All done behind my back while the cat's away. Well, I didn't say a word, you see. Just walked around the car a half dozen times with all of them watching me. Then I opened the door, grabbed it in both hands and tore it off its hinges. I took off my shoe and beat in the windshield, and kicked in the headlamps and the grill and every shiny red panel. And when that car was scattered all over the factory floor, I turned around and said, "Boys, you can have any color you want, as long as it's black." You know what Edsel said to me?

HARDING: No.

FORD: Nothing. What he always says. And that's his problem. He pats his men on the back like he's their nanny, not their boss, but that's Edsel, he just swallows it. Won't say a word. Sits there like a clam. Well,

I'll tell you something. You know the only thing that makes a clam worth something? A grain of sand. It gets inside that clam and irritates it, rubs it the wrong way, and the clam, well, he's got to fight back and coat that sand. And before you know it, the clam spits out a pearl. And that's why I keep at Edsel, 'cause I know he's got it in him.

HARDING (*pause*): Don't pearls come from oysters?

FORD: The point is, they're irritated! They make something out of nothing. Like I did. Like you did.

HARDING: I wouldn't say that.

FORD: I've been following your career, Mr. President. Absolutely fascinating. Teacher, insurance man, newspaper editor. And now President of the U.S. of A.

HARDING: Well, it is the land of opportunity, isn't it, Henry?

FORD: Yes it is. And you've taken advantage of so many along the way. (*Harding looks at him*) You don't have to be modest. I did my homework. My boys at the plant, my "Sociology Department," they're regular bloodhounds, they are. That's their job: personnel. Find out everything there is to know about a man. So when I told them we were taking a little trip together, they set right out after your trail. The whole bunch of them.

HARDING: And what did your dogs find, Henry?

FORD: They filled my ears, Warren. They filled them full.

(*Edison enters, annoyed*)

EDISON: I can't piss in these woods! It's getting so dark in there I can't see a thing! Some little animal could hop right up at you in the middle of your business.

FORD: I can turn the headlamps on.

EDISON: And then what, sell tickets? It's no use. I can't coordinate the operation anyway. Certain pieces of my anatomy resent the fact I'm still alive.

HARDING: Maybe we should try hiking back.

FORD: That's fine and dandy, but which way is back? Now that's west; there's the sunset.

HARDING: When we left, the sun was at our backs. So we were headed east.

FORD: All right then.

HARDING: But then you made a left.

FORD: So we went south.

HARDING: Or southeast.

FORD: Wait! Moss grows on the north side of a tree!

EDISON: That's not moss. It's green algae. And you're not Lewis and Clark. Face it, we're lost. We'd better take stock while we still have light.

(*Harding stops at the back of the car*)

HARDING: Let's see what we've got here in the trunk.

FORD: What do you think we've got? A bicycle with a compass?

HARDING: A lantern! That we can use. A tire iron . . . a hat!

EDISON (*putting on hat*): Insulation.

HARDING: Food!

EDISON: Food! That's the best news I've heard all day.

HARDING: A whole case full!

FORD: Pounded carrots.

HARDING: A case of pounded carrots?

21

FORD: They're good for you! Smartest food there is for your heart and eyes.

EDISON: What have we got for my stomach?

HARDING: What's this? An old cylinder phonograph! (*Pulls out an old wind-up machine*)

FORD (*irritated*): That's a gift for Mr. Edison. A *surprise* gift. (*To Edison*) It's one of your Vitaphones. We got it back to mint condition.

HARDING (*pulling out cylinders of music*): Songs, too. Gilbert and Sullivan! Enrico Caruso!

EDISON: Caruso!

FORD: You don't like Caruso?

EDISON: Every sob from that man sounds like it's shot from a cannon. You got a blanket in there?

HARDING: No.

EDISON (*shivering*): Perfect. Tonight we can listen to *Pagliacci* as we freeze to death.

FORD: We should get a fire going. It will keep us warm and signal we're here. When I was a boy, I could build one in two shakes of a lamb's tail. (*Takes tire iron*) I got the steel, all I need's a piece of flint and a pile of tinder.

EDISON: You don't even need that. Get a stick, notch a piece of wood and rub the stick between our hands 'til we get a spark going.

FORD: If I can find the right rock, this will be quicker.

EDISON: The kindling temperature for wood is only 469 degrees. And if we can locate some birch it wouldn't take any time at all.

(*Edison and Ford begin to look for sticks and wood. Harding pulls a match out of his pocket*)

HARDING: I've got a match.

FORD (*accusatory*): So you're a cigarette smoker?

HARDING: No, no. But I like an occasional cigar.

EDISON: And I like to keep the ice out of my veins. Bring it over here.

(*Ford and Edison combine their twigs and kindling*)

FORD: We'll have a fire roaring in no time.

HARDING: They'll spot us for sure now.

FORD: What say I splash a little gasoline on it first?

EDISON: You want to blow us back to camp?

FORD (*trying to light match; it goes out*): Aw shit. (*Tries another*) Aw shit.

EDISON: Let me try it.

FORD: Here! Got it, got it, aw shit.

EDISON: You've got to cover the flame!

FORD: I did, didn't you see me? I burned my hand!

HARDING: Men? Why don't we light the lantern first, and start the fire from that.

(*Ford and Edison look at each other, embarrassed they didn't think of it*)

FORD: That could work.

EDISON: We have one match left.

HARDING: Don't give it to me.

FORD: Mr. Edison?

(*Edison reluctantly takes it, lights the match, bending over it, lights the lantern as all hold their breath*)

EDISON: Here she goes . . . come on, come on. Yes! (*Ford and Harding cheer, clap Edison on the back*) I don't want *anyone* to ever hear about this.

HARDING: We need more kindling.

(*Ford picks up the book Edison was reading*)

EDISON: Put it down, Henry.

FORD (*looking at title*): Sir Arthur Conan Doyle . . .

HARDING: A mystery! I love them.

FORD: *The World of the Supernatural.*

EDISON: It's a mystery why he wrote it. Sherlock Holmes couldn't find one clear thought in it.

HARDING: Then why are you reading it?

EDISON: It's the only kind of human folly I still enjoy. The kind I can toss across the room whenever I'm sick of it.

FORD (*excited*): You're building it, aren't you?

EDISON: I didn't say that, Henry.

FORD: You're thinking about it, then. Admit it!

HARDING: Building what?

FORD: I've been after Mr. Edison for years to invent a machine to contact the dead.

HARDING (*taken aback*): Well. Good luck to you.

EDISON: We can't build a fire, and the man thinks I can find an afterlife.

FORD: If anybody can do it, you can.

HARDING: I don't know which would be more terrifying. Finding it, or not finding it.

EDISON: That all depends on who's waiting for you when you get there.

(*Harding smiles; Ford turns on him*)

FORD: You're not a believer, I take it.

HARDING: I certainly am. I most definitely am . . . well, yes and no.

EDISON: Good God . . . is there politics after death?

FORD (*burrowing in*): You believe in the human soul? The indestructible, eternal, all-knowing human soul?

HARDING (*pause*): Well, sure.

FORD: You'd better! You've got one right there under your vest. Some of us have old souls, some have young souls. But we've all got one. Standard equipment. Me; now I know I've been here before. I died once in the Civil War, and that's a fact. Why do you think I hate war so much? I've been there. I was born July 30, 1863, right after the Battle of Gettysburg. And one of those dead boys slipped me the soul I've been using ever since.

EDISON: So who needs a machine to contact the dead if you keep showing up anyhow?

FORD: Not every soul gets a second go-round! There's lots of them who can't make it back into a body, so they're still out there, all around us. Actual entities of force, intelligence—call them electrons if you like.

HARDING: All right.

FORD: When a man's doing good, these electrons swarm all around him like bees. They've helped Thomas Edison, they've helped Henry Ford. (*Pause*) They might have even helped you.

HARDING: Really.

FORD: That's right! The problem is, we rush around too much most of the time to let them help us. We want results, we want 'em now and we don't even let them get a toehold.

EDISON: That's all I need. To be sued by an electron.

FORD (*to Harding, indicating Edison*): He can scoff all
he likes, but he knows I'm right. Why do you think
he's reading that book? I've seen souls at work; I've
seen 'em and so have you. You know when a man's
all caught up in what he's doing, when he's concen-
trating so hard he loses himself? Loses time, where
he is, *who* he is even? He shuts himself off from the
world, this world, at least; that's when they come.
Call them what you want, call them particles, mole-
cules or creative inspiration, but I'll tell you what
they really are: spare souls with nowhere to go but
you.

(*The fire flares up; all jump back*)

EDISON: Christ in garters!

FORD: What was that?

HARDING: My flask. It fell in the fire.

FORD: You took my eyebrows off!

HARDING: I'm sorry.

FORD: You should be.

EDISON: You look better without eyebrows.

(*Harding begins with a jocularity that belies his true
concern*)

HARDING: You know, Mr. Ford. I might be one of your spare souls myself soon.

FORD: What are you talking about?

HARDING: I've been told I have two years to live. That doesn't even take me to the end of my term.

EDISON: Who told you that?

HARDING: Madame Marçia. Washington's premiere fortuneteller. She gave that cheerful piece of news to my wife. Who was only too happy to pass it on to me.

FORD: You don't believe her, do you?

HARDING: Of course not. I didn't believe her when she predicted I'd be elected to Congress. And I certainly didn't believe her when she forecast I'd be President. The Duchess brought the cards home to show me: Mars, the Sun and something about the Eighth House of the Zodiac. The House of Death. Unexpected, violent or unusual death.

FORD: That's grade-A cowcrap. Gypsy hoo-ha. Pay her more and she'll swear you'll live forever.

HARDING: Two weeks ago I was looking out the window of my office and a bolt of lightning shot from the sky onto the lawn, not fifty feet from my desk. Right

29

where I had been standing not an hour ago, in the White House backyard, during my handshake hour.

EDISON: Your what?

HARDING: My daily reception, I call it Handshake Hour. Everyday, twelve-thirty to lunch, no matter what's on the schedule, I go out and say how do you do.

EDISON: You greet diplomats in the backyard?

HARDING: No, not diplomats. People. Folks come by from all over the country, all over the world, you'd be surprised. I've had whole towns come to visit. Sometimes I'll stroll out and there'll be two thousand people on line.

FORD: You shake every hand?

HARDING: Yes, sir; I must have shaken half a million so far.

EDISON: I trust you don't let your other Presidential duties get in the way, then.

HARDING (*smiling*): Mr. Edison, you might not think it matters much, but I have to say, it's the most pleasant part of the job. I love to meet people. I have fun talking with them, even if it's just "Well, look who's here!" and that kind of thing. And they seem to enjoy it. I bring Laddie out, my Airedale. The day of the storm, we had a whole lawn filled with Girl Scouts in uniform. And the Duchess, too, she put hers on; her cap and kneesocks. So, frankly, I wasn't too upset when it started to rain. But when I saw that lightning! It scorched a hole in the ground, right where I'd been standing. It was like an explosion, like a white hot finger from the sky. The staff was scared to death, made me move my desk clear across the room. But I knew I was safe. Somehow, when the end does come, I don't think I'll go as quickly as a bolt of lightning. I have never been what you'd call a lucky man.

(*Sound offstage*)

FORD: What's that?

EDISON: The deer.

HARDING: He's still alive!

FORD: He shouldn't be . . .

HARDING: Good God. We can't let him suffer like this.

FORD: Nothing we can do about it.

HARDING: We can hit him with something. Put him out of his misery. (*Harding pulls up a rock no bigger than a fist*) This might do it.

FORD: You want to play catch with him?

EDISON: Why don't you crank up your Caruso? Four rounds of *Pagliacci* and the deer will kill himself.

(*Ford grabs the tire iron*)

FORD: Here you go. You can take him out with this.

HARDING: *I* can?

FORD: You're the one worried about him.

HARDING: That's right. But I thought since you were the man behind the wheel—

FORD: If *you* two had kept your eyes open—

EDISON: We did! We yelled to you! You'd still be driving, with the deer in the backseat!

FORD: Fine then! I'm a Michigan farmboy. Chicken or deer, it doesn't matter to me. One snap of the neck and it's done! (*Takes back the tire iron*) If you can't do your job, I will—

HARDING (*taking it back*): I can do my job!

FORD: Well, I haven't seen it! (*Harding and Ford stare at each other, then Harding turns, starts out, stops*) What are you waiting for? Lightning to hit him?

(*Harding turns back*)

HARDING: Mr. Ford, why don't we get this over with.

EDISON: Hit him at the base of the skull. That should be the most painless.

HARDING: I'm not talking about the deer. I'm talking about the reason I was invited here. (*To Ford*) You want the Muscle Shoals Hydroelectric Plant. And you expect me to convince Congress to sell it to you at a bargain rate. Isn't that what you want? "Henry"?

FORD: You know what I want? I want this country to learn to harness its own energy. I want to give jobs to every man and woman who needs one. I want the farmers of the Tennessee Valley to be able to plant the richest farmland since the garden of Eden. That's what I want.

HARDING: And your price?

FORD: This isn't about money, can't you see that? You've got a half-built plant sitting there like a dead stump, no use to anybody! If Wilson didn't give up on it when the war ended it could be in full swing by now! Have you ever *seen* the Tennessee River, Harding? Do you have any idea how much energy we could collar down there?

HARDING: I've read the figures . . .

FORD (*interrupting*): I wrote them! We could be running three to four hundred nitrate factories on that land! Three to four hundred! We could be stockpiling the largest supply of fertilizer and gunpowder on this planet. Enough for every crop and bomb this country could ever use. We can take the Tennessee Valley and turn it into another Detroit!

(*Edison takes up his book*)

EDISON: Where was I . . . ?

HARDING: I understand the possibilities—

FORD: These aren't "possibilities"! These are facts, just waiting for us to open our eyes! We're sitting on unlimited power! And the next time we've got ourselves a war, we don't have to go with our hat in our hands to every nancy boy in Europe begging for firepower! We can drop bombs over the whole damn planet! And they'll know it, and line up begging for vegetables instead! Don't you see what this means, Harding? We can do an epochal thing here! An epochal thing! We can eliminate war from the world!

EDISON (*closing book*): How's that, Henry? Blow us all to bits and then scrape us up for fertilizer?

FORD: You go ahead and laugh, but I know we can do it. I believe in people. Not like you cynical sons of bitches who don't believe in souls or solutions. I believe we can lick any problem we set our minds to. And so does every Joe in the Tennessee Valley. They want me, you know that? They're naming streets after me, they're handing out Ford buttons.

HARDING: You've promised them so much, who can blame them?

FORD: I haven't promised anything I can't deliver.

HARDING: A seventy-five-mile-long city of hydroelectric dams and factories. They don't see water in that river, they see dollar bills—

FORD: So do I! That's what's there! A river of energy dollars!

HARDING: . . . And Henry Ford standing on the banks like Moses, promising to part the seas—

FORD: Damn right! Before you drown the poor bastards in taxes and red tape.

HARDING: I resent that.

FORD (*sarcastic*): Well, don't I feel terrible. The truth is, Mr. President, that the reason for all the foot dragging is that none of your boys can figure out yet how they can carve their own slice of the pie.

HARDING: The truth, Mr. Ford, is that the operation is nowhere near as simple as you make it out to be—

FORD: You bet it is! It's too simple! That's why you're all scratching your heads.

HARDING: We are considering every proposal submitted to us—

FORD: Don't consider! Do something! Just for once, I'd like to see a politician do something for the people and not his own pocket! Believe it or not, Harding, there's some of us left who still love this country, and not just 'cause it's a string of letters on a dollar bill. There's some of us who still remember when our Capitol was Washington D.C., and not Wall Street. I want Muscle Shoals and I'm going to get it, with or without you. But you remember this, Harding; if you're not my friend, you're my enemy. (*Ford grabs the tire iron*) Now get out of my way so I can do your job for you. (*Ford exits towards the deer*)

HARDING (*pause*): So there it is. (*Turns to Edison*) Mr. Edison—

EDISON: I can't help you.

HARDING: I'm not asking you to take sides—

EDISON: I already have. I'm on my own side.

(*Ford enters*)

FORD (*to Harding*): He's no friend of yours, Harding. (*The men turn to him*) The deer's dead.

HARDING: Good. Good for him.

EDISON: Henry, I want you to be clear on something, too. I'm no friend of yours, either.

FORD: Of course you are. Why would you say a thing like that?

EDISON: We are social acquaintances. We see each other on a regular basis because we welcome the company of someone who's not afraid of us and doesn't want something. But this is not a social situation, and this is one ride you can't talk me into taking. All my life I've never gotten involved in politics, and I'm not senile enough to start now.

HARDING: I'm going to walk back.

FORD: You don't know where you're going!

HARDING: So you've said. But frankly, I'd prefer to be alone.

EDISON: You are; have a seat.

FORD: You start tramping through that forest, you're going to get lost or run smack into some hungry grizzly.

EDISON: Or Democrat.

HARDING: I'll take my chances with the grizzly. (*Starts to go; Ford goes to him*)

FORD: Listen here. Alright, then. Maybe I said some things I shouldn't have—

EDISON: You, Henry?

FORD: We're out here and we've got to stick together 'til somebody finds us. And as far as Muscle Shoals—

HARDING: The subject is closed; I won't hear another word about it.

FORD: That's fine with me, sir. That's just fine. There's plenty of other subjects you and I can talk about.

(*Harding looks at Ford; Edison intervenes*)

EDISON: If we want to be found, we should build up this fire.

FORD: It's not much of a fire, that's for sure.

EDISON: Too much softwood. All we've got here is spruce and pine. Can't get a hot enough flame. What you've got to look for is hickory, oak, beech, sugar maple, white ash or birch.

HARDING: It's getting dark.

EDISON: Bring what you find. I'll sort it. I'd get up except my legs are either frozen or asleep, I'm not sure which.

(*Ford takes off his jacket*)

FORD: Here. Take this if you're cold.

EDISON: That's very generous, Henry. But I couldn't.

FORD: Go on; take it.

EDISON: Alright. (*Reaches for it; Ford holds it out*)

FORD: Friends do this kind of thing for each other.

(*Edison takes the coat*)

EDISON: If I ever decide I need one, I'll keep you in mind.

FORD: Oh, come on! You expect me to believe you never had one single friend your whole life?

HARDING (*calling back in*): What about your mother?

FORD: Mothers don't count. They'd pretend to like you even if they don't.

EDISON: My mother liked me until I was about four years old. She didn't know what to make of me after that. Neither did my father.

FORD: Well, what did you do? You had to do something.

EDISON: Get the wood, Henry.

FORD: Something had to happen—

HARDING: He doesn't want to talk about it! And frankly, I don't want to hear it!

(*This is enough to prod Edison*)

EDISON (*to Ford*): I set fire to my father's barn when I was four. Almost burned the whole town down; lucky there wasn't a wind.

FORD: Why did you do that?

EDISON: I wanted to see how fire worked. Turned out I discovered how my father operated, instead. He whipped me in the village square, in front of the whole town. I'm surprised he didn't give our neighbors a turn.

FORD: Every child does some fool thing. Heck, I used to make screwdrivers from the metal in my mother's corsets. She'd beat me when she caught me. Every single time.

HARDING: Why didn't you just stop?

FORD: I did. As soon as I got me a full set of tools.

EDISON: My mother believed I was born without feelings.

HARDING (*pause*): She told you that?

FORD: Why would she say such a thing?

EDISON: There was a boy I played with when we lived in Milan. He was six or seven, older than I was. His father owned the general store. I remember he always had a good suit of clothes. Not like mine. I wore hand-me-downs from my older brother, Carlile. Carlile died when he was six, but 'til I got there, his clothes fit me fine. One day this boy and I went for a swim in the creek. Outside of town, it was, in the woods. We took off our clothes and jumped right in; nobody else was there. And we played together, whatever boys play in the water. Dunking and hiding and holding our breath. But after awhile, I didn't see him. I waited for him to come up, but it got dark, so I put my clothes on and went home.

HARDING (*pause*): What happened then?

EDISON: I ate dinner. We had chicken stew. And then I went to bed. Until sometime in the middle of the night my mother shook me awake. The whole town was out with lanterns looking for the boy. And someone mentioned me. I told them how we swam and how I waited, and they went off to drag the creek for his body. Which they found. And that was that.

(*Ford and Harding exchange looks*)

HARDING: Why didn't you tell anyone?

EDISON: I did, when they asked.

HARDING: Before that, at dinner, when you got home.

FORD: He must have been terrified! Seeing a boy killed like that! No wonder you didn't say anything, you probably felt it was your fault somehow!

EDISON: I don't remember. I remember standing in the water. I remember how cold it was. And I can remember thinking, "He's not coming up. He must be drowned." And I was hungry, so I went home. To this day I can't remember his name. There's a good reason for that and I hope I never understand what it is. (*Sifts through wood Harding has brought*) Birch! Here's the ticket!

(*Edison adds to the fire. There is a pause; the men look into the darkness around them*)

HARDING: Somebody should have found us by now.

EDISON: The only one who saw us go was your Secret Service man. Unless he spread the word, everyone probably thinks we're sound asleep in our tents.

FORD: Not my wife. Not Edsel. I thought once it got dark, Edsel would come looking for me.

HARDING (*pause*): You did?

EDISON: I think he will, Henry. Before Christmas, definitely.

FORD: What about this Secret Service fella of yours? Is he good?

HARDING: Colonel Starling? I'd say he is. Got decorated for bravery at Château Thierry. Of course, that was war; I can't vouch for how good he is at hide and seek.

FORD (*snorting*): Soldiers. When I was a boy we called them by their rightful names: murderers. Said so right in our McGuffey Readers, written right across their chests.

EDISON: Be sure you mention that to the Colonel.

HARDING (*listening*): Hello.

FORD: You hear something?

HARDING: I thought I did.

(*All start shouting*)

ALL: Hello/Anybody there/Hello!

(*Pause; quiet, except for the call of an owl. They look at each other*)

FORD: I know what we do! (*Goes back to car*) I should have thought of this before. (*Ford takes out the old phonograph*) The phonograph! Keep it playing loud as she goes and sooner or later somebody will hear us. (*Looks at song cylinders*) Just the thing! (*Puts one on; we hear "Alexander's Ragtime Band"*)

EDISON: At least it should clear out any wildlife for miles around.

(*They listen; it's now harder to speak above the record. Edison picks up his book*)

FORD (*to Harding*): You and the Mrs. do much dancing?

HARDING: Can't say we do.

FORD: It's first-rate exercise. Not like these modern dances. All they're good for is making babies and money. That's why dance halls want their men and ladies smashed right up against each other, you know. Fits more folks on the dance floor. (*Calls*) Don't you think so, Mr. Edison?

EDISON (*not looking up from his book*): Can't hear you, Henry. Not for awhile.

FORD (*to Harding*): Wouldn't hurt you to start. It's the way to lose that belly, I can promise you that. You know what's good for a gut? "The Ripple." You know that one?

HARDING: No.

FORD: The Ripple—(*Ford, by himself, does a few moves, demonstrating; one hand up, one hand on his own belly*)

HARDING: That's not The Ripple.

FORD: I'll say it is!

HARDING: That's The Newport!

FORD: The what?

HARDING: The Newport! (*Harding demonstrates himself*) You go round like this . . .

(Ford joins in; both men are dancing separately)

FORD: That's right! What did you call it?

HARDING: The Newport.

(Edison looks up, disgusted)

FORD: Look at him. The man's a natural.

(Ford, Harding continue dancing)

EDISON: Next time you bring along my inventions, remember the electric chair.

FORD: "And if you care to hear the Swanee River
Played in Ragtime
Come on and Hear
Come on and Hear . . ."

HARDING and FORD: Alexander's Ragtime Band."

FORD: Let's go round again. *(Ford rewinds phonograph)*

HARDING: That's a first-rater.

FORD: A young kid wrote it. The one thing these Germans know is how to write music. You've got to give them that much.

EDISON: Irving Berlin's not German.

FORD: Berlin's not in Germany?

EDISON: Irving Berlin's an American Jew.

(*Ford stops the phonograph; pulls the cylinder off*)

FORD (*turning, smiling*): Is he? I didn't know.

HARDING (*pause*): Talented fella. Wrote lots of songs for the War effort.

FORD: Now here's some real American music. This is what folks should be dancing to, and don't tell me some Jew Boy wrote it! (*"Turkey in The Straw" can be heard; Ford claps*) First time I danced with Clara was at a square dance. Greenfield Dancing Club, New Year's Eve, 1888. Mr. Edison, let me show you some steps. Nothing better to keep your body in prime working order.

EDISON: This body has one purpose: to carry this head around.

FORD: You want to shake the chill, don't you? (*Starts to clap; turns to Harding*) How about you, "Mistuh Harding"?

HARDING: No, thank you.

FORD (*still clapping*): "Swing her high, swing her low, don't step on her pretty toe." Come on now! Promenade! (*Ford takes Harding's arm to swing around, Harding shakes him off*)

HARDING: I said no!

(*Ford looks at Harding, then after a moment, resumes clapping to the beat*)

FORD: Alright then. It just surprises me. I thought you'd be a dancing man, that's all. I thought it would be in your blood.

HARDING (*to Ford, furious*): Turn it off—

EDISON (*not paying attention*): What?

HARDING: TURN IT OFF! (*Harding lifts the needle*) I know what you're trying to do!

FORD: I'm trying to dance!

HARDING (*to Edison*): I know what he's insinuating! I've heard these stupid lies all my life.

FORD (*to Edison*): What's he talking about?

EDISON (*to Harding*): What are you talking about?

HARDING: He's implying I've got black blood in my veins. And he's not man enough to just come out and say it, face to face.

FORD: What's there to say? I don't see it's any of my business if your great-grandpa jumped the fence.

HARDING: Nobody "jumped the fence"! That's a hateful rumor William Chancellor started to keep me out of office! He never had a shred of proof.

FORD: I'd guess not. Not after your Republican Committee burned his press and his papers.

HARDING: Chancellor's a madman! He's a lunatic!

FORD: Then why'd you buy him off? Why not let him keep raving?

HARDING: I said he's a lunatic, I didn't say people won't listen to him! He's a one-man circus, they'll pack the tent! But I don't have to stand for the poisonous slander of a contemptible bigot! Not from him and not from you. (*Harding starts to go*)

FORD: Are you calling me a bigot?

HARDING: Yes!

FORD (*stopping Harding*): Do you have any idea how many colored men I have working for me? Negro workers *and* Negro bosses, do you have any idea?

HARDING: No I don't, and I don't care either.

FORD: Then you're the bigot! Because I do care! And I don't have anything but respect for the Negro! They're good men and good workers, and if you're the first black President, hip hip hooray! It's just a pity you're so ashamed of it.

HARDING (*pause*): Perhaps I misunderstood what you were saying.

FORD: Perhaps you did.

HARDING: I hope we can forget all about this.

FORD: I hope so, too.

HARDING: I don't see any purpose to holding a grudge—

FORD: There is none! I'm agreeing with you! And I'll work at it. Because I've got one of those memories that's like a curse; it holds on like bad teeth. Now you take most people; they don't have that problem. I envy them. You take that rumor about you being partial to the Dark Continent? Right or wrong, true or false, it didn't matter; they forgot long before election day. (*Harding looks at him*) You know it doesn't matter to me! I told you that! But Mr. President, between us? If you ever want to know for sure? And I admit, I'm a man who doesn't like to leave a cow half-milked. If you're ever curious I can turn my Sociology Boys loose on it. And they'll find out. (*Snaps fingers*) Quicker than that.

HARDING (*pause*): So what's your offer, Mr. Ford? How much for Muscle Shoals?

FORD: I'll pay a fair price. Five million dollars.

HARDING: Five million? Muscle Shoals cost the taxpayers over eighty million so far!

FORD: What's it worth now? Not the change in my pocket.

HARDING: Ten million if we scrap it completely and sell the property.

FORD: Nobody will pay that and you know it. Five million. And before I put that up I want the whole operation renovated. I'm not going to pay for anything that won't work.

HARDING: You can't be serious! Do you know what it would cost to restore the dam and the factories? Fifty, sixty million dollars!

EDISON (*putting book away*): Maybe I can explain this more clearly: ALL Henry's asking is that you sell him your eighty-million-dollar assets for five million dollars. But he's also giving you the opportunity to spend another fifty million to fix them first.

FORD: That's right.

EDISON: Henry, not even the government can waste that kind of money.

FORD: I'm not the one who closed my eyes and let the dam and the plant fall to pieces in the first place. Same thing they're doing to the whole country.

EDISON: But you can save it.

FORD: You bet I can. Good government's as simple as good business. If it works, keep with it and if it don't, it's tomorrow's trash. That goes for politics and politicians. (*To Harding*) Five million. Non-negotiable.

HARDING: Your proposal makes no sense!

FORD: No sense? You're standing here telling *me* about sense? You wouldn't know "sense" if it bit your ass and sang happy birthday!

EDISON: Stop it, Henry.

FORD: No, I won't stop. Because I'm right and you know it.

HARDING: I don't have to listen to this.

FORD: No, you're too busy listening to Harry Daugherty and his forty thieves who ran you in the first place! So they can tell you what to hear and say and think and hop in your pocket for a free ride to Washington! Two-bit crooks hiding behind a haircut and a handshake and a Santy Claus voice, and if it wasn't for women getting the vote, Cox would be President and you'd be kissing babies in Ohio!

HARDING: That's enough—

FORD: You bet it's enough! I can't stand more lies! I can't stand the stupidity! You know who calls your shots the same as I do! Your Wall Street Boys! Sons of bitches who never made anything in their whole life except money, bastards with bank accounts instead of brains who bought you your job.

HARDING: Ford, I don't care what you think about me. You can say anything you want about Warren Harding. But I won't stand for you abusing the office of the President—

FORD: Abusing the office? You beat me to it!

HARDING: I'm walking back.

FORD: Abusing the office and the office closet! (*Harding stops*) Nice thing about White House closets, they're nice and roomy. Don't you think so, "Wurren"? Big enough to fit two people, even. Especially if one of them's just an itty-bitty thing. Say sixteen years old.

HARDING: You're a liar.

FORD: You're right, she was sixteen when you met her. My mistake. Nan's nineteen, now, isn't she? All grown up. I know she's old enough to be a Mommy. Cute little thing, her baby girl, Elizabeth Ann. Fat little cheeks, big blue eyes, just like yours. You should see her, "Wurren." You really should.

HARDING: She is none of your business.

FORD: I think she is. I think it's everybody's business, when the President turns the White House into a cathouse. Don't you think so, Mr. Edison?

EDISON: I'm not listening, Henry.

(*Ford approaches Harding*)

FORD: Flopping around on the floor of his coatroom, rolling over the galoshes with a girl young enough to be his daughter, the President of the United States, with his whore and his bastard baby—

(*Harding goes to hit him; Ford ducks it, assumes fighting pose*)

HARDING: You keep away from them, do you hear me?

FORD: Don't threaten me, Harding!

EDISON: STOP IT! Both of you! You're a couple of old jackasses!

(*Both men pull back*)

HARDING (*to Ford*): You are a vicious, twisted man.

FORD: I'm a man who knows the truth and how to use
it.

HARDING: You're not getting Muscle Shoals, no matter
what you do. You can take me down, but you're not
getting your greedy hands on that. I'll stop you any
way I can.

FORD: You do that! Take time out of your Handshake
Hour and come right at me! Because there won't be
any more folks lining up on your front lawn to say
hello! They'll be lining up to run you out of town on
a rail, with the Duchess and her Girl Scouts leading
the charge.

HARDING: I will fight you all the way—

EDISON: You won't win, you know that. (*Harding looks
at Edison*) Use your head. Give him the damn factories.

FORD: This isn't just about the factories!

EDISON (*furious*): What else do you want?

FORD: I want to knock some rust off this government! I
want to give it back to the people and boot the

moneychangers out of the temple so fast it will make
their heads spin. The shylocks and the socialists who
don't believe in an honest day's work, and suck our
teats instead. I want the big boss at the front desk
with his pants on, that's what I want! I want to fix
this country and put it back on the road again, and
that's why I'm going to be the thirtieth President of
the United States!

EDISON: What?!

HARDING: Good God. (*Harding and Edison stare at
Ford; there is a sound in the bushes*) Someone's here
—(*Harding moves off*) Hello! Hello? (*Harding exits*)

FORD (*to Edison*): I want your help, Mr. Edison. I'm
counting on it.

(*Edison looks at Ford as Harding rushes back in*)

HARDING: The deer's alive!

FORD: He can't be!

HARDING: He's trying to get up!

EDISON (*to Ford*): I thought you killed him!

FORD: I never said that—

HARDING: You said you killed him!

FORD: I said he was dead! I didn't have to kill him!

HARDING: Didn't you check? Didn't you see if he was breathing?

FORD: He wasn't breathing.

EDISON: What was he doing? Holding his breath?

HARDING: First you hit him, then you let him suffer like this!

FORD: I'll take care of him!

EDISON: So do it!

FORD: I WILL! (*Ford grabs tire iron and exits. A moment later, he steps back into view*)

EDISON: Now what?

FORD: He keeps looking at me.

EDISON: What does that matter?

FORD: You want him to bite me?

EDISON: I want him to learn how to drive.

(*Ford exits. We hear a scuffling*)

FORD (*offstage*): The damn animal won't stay still!

HARDING: Hold him down!

FORD (*re-entering*): You hold him down!

HARDING: I'll do that!

(*Harding charges offstage; Ford follows. Edison watches*)

FORD (*offstage*): You ready?

HARDING (*offstage*): Not yet.

FORD (*offstage*): Get behind him.

HARDING (*offstage*): He keeps turning . . .

EDISON: Damnation.

FORD (*offstage*): Grab his leg . . .

HARDING (*offstage*): This leg?

FORD (*offstage*): Any leg!

HARDING (*offstage*): Got it!

FORD (*offstage*): Hold on!

HARDING (*offstage*): I can't!

FORD (*offstage*): Move over!

HARDING (*offstage*): I *did!*

FORD (*offstage*): Here we go, on a count of three . . .
one, two . . .

(*Edison, during this exchange, has gotten out the Caruso cylinder and slipped it onto the Vitaphone. He turns the machine on and lays the needle down. As the offstage melee escalates, we hear the start of "Ridi Pagliacci" over the cries of anguish from Ford and Harding, the volume rising dramatically after Ford's "two." Edison turns the Vitaphone so the horn is directed offstage towards the men, sits down and covers his ears and turns away as the lights fade. End of Act One.*)

Act Two

ACT II

Lights up reveals Edison staring into the fire, Harding stretched out on the ground, eyes closed, and Ford, his back to us, rummaging in the car while he speaks. Twenty minutes have passed.

FORD: Most people dig their graves with their own teeth. They take better care of their cars than their own bodies and that's all we are, machines on ten toes . . . (*Ford turns, walks back toward the fire; he has a blood-spotted white bandage, made out of his shirt sleeve, wrapped around his head. He walks back with a slight limp, carrying a large can that he's secured to a Y-shaped tree branch. He heats the can as he talks*) . . . stamped out of blood and bones. So what do we pour down our tanks? Slop and poisons; no wonder we break down! What do you think causes sickness and craziness and crime? A bellyful of the wrong fuel! Vegetables!! There's your answer. And carrots; carrots are the crowned heads of the vegetable kingdom! The color of good health is orange! (*Leans in over fire; his back suddenly locks*) Aw shit; I'm locked.

(*Edison rises to help him; Harding opens his eyes*)

HARDING: Is he alright?

EDISON: His back's out again.

(*Harding sits up, looks offstage*)

HARDING: How's the deer?

FORD: The deer's fine! The deer's jim dandy! I'm the one you nearly killed!

HARDING: The deer kicked me!

FORD: You knocked me off balance!

HARDING: You hit your own leg!

EDISON (*to Harding*): You feeling better?

HARDING: He knocked the wind out of me, alright. That was some kick. Look at that; he's sitting up. He looks livelier than we do.

FORD: 'Course he does! He got revenge. He kicked you, chased me; I bet if he got a good shot at Edison, that deer would be dancing by now.

EDISON: His hind leg's broken. When he tried to get up, I could see that much.

FORD: Who wants carrots? (*No response*) Come on now! They're tasty, too. Barbecued carrot patties. I think we can squeeze some juice out of the leftovers. (*Approaches Edison*) Go on, grab a handful. You said you were hungry.

John Cunningham as Henry Ford *(seated, front)*, Ken Howard as Warren G. Harding *(standing)* and Robert Prosky as Thomas A. Edison *(seated, back)*.

Photos of the 1995 Off-Broadway production at the Lucille Lortel Theatre by Joan Marcus

Ken Howard *(center)* with John Cunningham *(right)* and Robert Prosky *(left)*.

John Cunningham *(seated, right)* with Robert Prosky.

Ken Howard *(center)* with John Cunningham *(right)* and Robert Prosky *(left)*.

EDISON: I did. And when I get hungry enough to hallucinate they're not pounded carrots, I'll dig right in.

FORD (*to Harding*): How about you?

HARDING: No, thank you.

FORD: You've got to keep up your strength.

HARDING: I will.

FORD: Just a taste—

HARDING: I said no!

EDISON: Stop it! Both of you! (*Pause*) Good God, I have children again.

HARDING (*taking a patty*): Maybe the deer will eat them.

(*Harding exits; Ford calls after him*)

FORD: If it wasn't for you, he'd be out of his misery by now!

EDISON: Don't underestimate your carrots.

(*Offstage, Harding makes baby talk to the deer*)

FORD (*watching Harding offstage*): Look at him. He's talking to the damn animal. The man's not even fit to be a Vice President.

EDISON: Let me see your head. (*Ford sits down. Edison examines his head*)

FORD: This is all his fault, too.

EDISON: You ran into the tree, Henry. Head first. You can't blame that on him.

FORD: He's the one who screamed. I thought the deer was charging me.

EDISON: The deer barely stood up. You jumped ten feet. You look fine. You've got a hard head. What a surprise.

FORD: That man shouldn't be running a country, he should be running a zoo.

EDISON: The question is, should you be President of one?

FORD: Why shouldn't I?

EDISON: Henry, you've tried politics before! Look what happened when you ran for the Senate—

FORD: I didn't run! I let them put my name on the ballot! I never made a single speech and I almost won!

EDISON: Because you *didn't* make a single speech! You're a terrible speaker, and you know it! You trip over your own tongue the minute there's six people in the room. It's embarrassing. You can't campaign, Henry! The Democrats don't need a second jackass.

FORD: Except this time I want to win. And me talking, that's just a problem to solve. I'll lick it. I'll pay for the best people to tell me what to say and how to say it! It's just square dancing all over again, don't you see that? You buy the best band, you learn the steps and then you just move with the music!

EDISON: And fall flat on your face.

FORD (*irritated*): So what? You think that's the worst thing that can happen? It's not. The worst thing's not falling; the worst thing's standing at the punch bowl all night with your hands in your pockets. What do you say, Mr. Edison? I need to know. Are you with me or against me?

EDISON: Think of me as Switzerland. Cold and neutral.

FORD: Then you're with me.

EDISON: That's not what I said.

FORD: No, you didn't. But the way I look at it, that's pretty much the same thing.

(Harding returns, wiping his hands off)

HARDING: He ate! He licked away at it when I put it in front of him. I thought he'd bite me, but he didn't.

FORD: Oh good, you've got a pet. If you ask me, it's a waste of carrots. If his leg is busted, he's a goner.

HARDING *(ignoring him)*: I should have known I couldn't watch you hit him. When I was a boy we had Butchering Season. We'd slaughter all the livestock to get ready for winter. I was no good at it then, and I'm no good at it now. I guess I've never had much of a killer instinct. I envy you that, Mr. Ford, I truly do.

FORD: Forget the deer five minutes, can you do that? I think we have more important things to talk about.

HARDING: We do.

EDISON: Where's my book?

FORD: Let's look at the facts. Fact one: I'm going to be the next President. With or without your help. Fact two is that I want Muscle Shoals, and I want it now because I don't want it looking like any conflict of interest later on. *(Edison looks up from his book, incredulous)* Those are actualities, pure and simple. The only thing you have to decide is how much mud we throw at each other 'til we get there. And you can read a popularity poll the same as I can. The truth is

I'm the most popular man in this country. More popular than you, more popular than anybody. (*Turns*)
No offense, Mr. Edison.

EDISON: I'm sulking, Henry.

FORD (*to Harding*): So this is what you do. Hand over
Muscle Shoals now. Push it past Congress before
they even blink and, if anybody says "Boo," believe
me, I have the boys to scare 'em back, don't you
worry.

HARDING: I'm reassured.

FORD: Don't get huffy with me, Harding. You've got
something to say, just say it.

HARDING: I do—

FORD: I'm not done yet! The second thing you do is
even easier. You don't run in '24. You throw your
support my way; everything you've got.

HARDING: You're a Democrat!

FORD: You think only Democrats drive my cars? They'll
all vote for me, anybody who ever pushed their gas
pedal to the floor. And I don't care who they run
against me, either. I'll beat anybody except Jesus
Christ, and that includes his folks, Mary and Joe.

HARDING: It's not that simple.

FORD: I've got the money to make it simple. You run an election the same way you run a business. Throw two men in the same job, same title, same office and see which one walks out of it alive. So it's your call. We can work on the same team or I can hunker down with our newspaper boys. And by the time I'm through with you, you won't be able to swing a vote in Sodom or Gomorrah. (*Pause*) What'll it be?

HARDING: You've given me a lot to think about. I was trying to do that before, laying here. Much too much to think about. So after awhile I thought I should listen to my heart—

FORD: "Listen to your heart." Talk like a man, Harding, don't throw flowers at me.

HARDING: I've been a politician most my life, Henry. Saying what I really think, well, that's not a skill I've had to develop. But here it is: I think you should go to the press.

FORD: What?

EDISON: Don't be a damn fool!

HARDING: No, no; I think if anybody ever rescues us from this wilderness, you should grab a reporter and give him the story of his life. Henry Howard at the

Post is a favorite of mine; he can even write. Why
don't you tell him?

FORD: Did you get kicked in the head?

HARDING: Maybe I did. Maybe he kicked some sense
into me.

EDISON: You know, we've got the timber here. Maybe
you should just hammer a cross together and take a
shortcut.

HARDING: You don't understand—

EDISON: It's self-pitying nonsense! If you don't want to
fight him for the damn office, you can just step aside!

FORD: Don't you realize what this would do to you?
They'll be all over you, swinging their hatchets!
You'll have no job and no marriage! Why do that to
yourself?

HARDING: Because I don't want to be President. Or
married. I never did. If you want the job, go ahead
and take it. I wish you could do the same with my
wife.

EDISON: But he doesn't have to "take it"!

FORD: I can run in the next election! I told you that!

HARDING: I know what you told me. And I know myself, much better than you gentlemen do. When I walk out of these woods, all I'll ever decide to do is procrastinate. You said it yourself, and you were right. Other people will decide for me. But here, I can make the decision I know is right. Go to the press. Tell them what I am. They'll boot me out the front door and so will my wife. You'll be the President, and I'll be the happiest man on earth.

FORD: Now just hold on here—

EDISON: Why don't you just boot your wife out? Seems the easiest solution.

HARDING: I couldn't do it. Never could, since she popped the question. I'm a boy who can't say no.

FORD: But if she knew about this girlfriend of yours, if you told her on the sly—

HARDING: You think she doesn't know? She knows about Nan. I'm sure she even knows about the baby. I think she even knew about Carrie Phillips, too. Carrie and her husband Jim were our best friends back in Blooming Grove, they lived right down the street. I'm surprised your Sociology boys missed Carrie, Mr. Ford. I thought everybody knew about her.

FORD (*caught off guard*): Carrie Phillips, you say . . .

HARDING: I can fill you in. But the Duchess knows. The woman's fought for what she's got and she'll want to hold on to it. Right now she's the wife of the President of the United States. I'm simply an accessory to that fact. You know, I just realized if we tell the reporters now, I won't even have to worry about Muscle Shoals. That will be the Vice President's problem. (*Pleased*) You'll have to talk it out with Mr. Coolidge. "Silent Cal." Good luck to you. Last month at dinner the Speaker's wife made a bet she could get more than two words out of him. Calvin looked up from his soup and said, "You lose." (*Harding laughs, enjoying himself*)

EDISON (*to Ford*): What have you done?

HARDING: Don't blame Henry. A lot of what he said about me was right. And what about you, Mr. Edison? You never voted for me, did you?

EDISON (*pause*): No. I voted for Cox.

HARDING: So did I! (*Harding laughs as Ford and Edison look at each other*) I never wanted the job in the first place! I was happy enough in the Senate. And to tell you the truth, I was never convinced I belonged there either. But there was worse than me, and I wasn't hurting anybody. Show up to roll call, try to get along with both teams and play poker Tuesdays and Thursdays. That was fine. That I could do. You know what did me in? I look like a President.

FORD: If you didn't want the job, why'd you let them run you at all?

HARDING: I tried to back out, all through the convention! Nobody would hear about it. Least of all Harry Daugherty, my campaign manager. I begged Harry. I told him I wasn't the man for the job. I wasn't big enough. I even told him I had a way out of it: all we had to do is tell somebody in Wilson's camp about my times in the hospital. Another thing your boys missed, Henry. I was in the Battle Creek Sanitarium five times, starting way back when, before I got married. You can bring that to the newspaper boys, too. We always put out that it was poor health, that I got run down. But it wasn't my body. I would just get to a point that I couldn't even move, I felt so . . . so sad. I couldn't brush my teeth without thinking that in fifty years, they'll be cracking underground. I couldn't say hello to my best friends because what I was really thinking was I don't know them at all. They're just more strangers, but I know their names. Nervous breakdowns. That's what they called them. But Dr. Kellogg always put me back together again. And then I'd be back in business for awhile, until the next time. And Harry Daugherty, of course, he knew all about it, but he wouldn't hear of me telling anybody. The funny thing is: A month before the election, I got so damn scared I went to one of Wilson's boys myself. Someone from home I knew I could trust. And he told me they knew. They knew all along, but Wilson wouldn't let them use it. The man should never have been in politics. I told Daugherty, I'm not a President. I'm not a great man. And he said, "Warren, greatness is a thing of the past. It's an illusion. There are no first-raters out there now, and you're the best of the second rate. So you're it. You're going to run and you're going to win." It was like I was doing a favor for everybody who was running me. I became the President of the United States as a favor. HELLO! (*No sounds*) First thing I'd do if I were you, Henry, is to get yourself a new Secret Service.

FORD: You're not dumping all your dirty work on me, Harding. I am not going to tell the newspapers that you have a ladyfriend, a love child, a cabinet full of crooks and chiselers and you're crazy as a loon to boot! What would I look like? Some kind of cripple kicker!

HARDING: You have a point.

FORD: One scandal's enough. More than that, the papers won't ever get it straight.

HARDING: Nan and the baby ought to do the trick. Maybe even just Nan, if you don't mind. She'd love to see her name in the paper, I betcha. I can even give you some pictures—

FORD: Would you stop being so damned cheerful about it!

75

HARDING: Sorry. But you are doing me a favor. Do you know, I've never gotten one look at the little girl. And she's two years old now. Nan is always after me. She said she'd wheel her in a carriage past my window, I could just peek out, but I won't let her. I've never even seen the kid's picture. Nan's sent plenty, but Daugherty's boys in the mailroom make them disappear. They burn them, would you believe it? They're all so afraid of losing their jobs. Nan says she looks just like me, the poor thing. Not that I would have looked at the pictures, even if I got them. I knew I couldn't. If I saw her I'd have to touch her, you know, and hold her. It would have been all over. But now, Henry, thanks to you, it is. You're giving me a whole new life. And my little girl . . . (*Harding chokes up, turns away*) Excuse me.

(*Harding exits*)

EDISON: Terrifying. What we pretend is civilization.

FORD: And what's that supposed to mean?

EDISON: Do you realize how little he needs to be happy?

FORD: He's a five-nut fruitcake!

EDISON: You're the one who wants his job.

FORD: That's right! And after listening to him, I've never wanted anything more in my life! The sooner the better! Can you imagine a President with honest-to-God ideas and the spunk to make them work? This country won't know what hit it!

EDISON: Neither did the deer.

FORD: Mr. Edison, I've never said this to you before. But all your naysaying, all the sneering when a fella wants to make a difference in the world; it's so easy. It really is. So much easier than rolling up your sleeves and taking a whack at the problem to fix it.

EDISON: Machines can be fixed, not men, Henry. I'm not sure whether we're over-designed or under-equipped, but I know we're unfixable.

FORD: Look, I can see how you feel; I get sore myself! You know you have an answer, and everybody is either too scared or stupid to take a chance and change things—

EDISON: I don't have any answers—

FORD: Sure you do! Look what just happened with this war we got ourselves in! How many boys did we lose when we didn't have to? How many times did you and I try to talk to the bullet heads in the State Department, who couldn't even borrow the brains to understand what we were talking about! Well, those boys will be the first casualties when I take over. We can take an axe to a whole forest of dead wood, and I want you in there swinging with me—

EDISON: No, Henry . . .

FORD: The country needs you! I need you! Secretary of State, Secretary of Agriculture. Secretary of Defense, if you like that. Take your pick.

EDISON: Not interested.

FORD: How 'bout the patent office? You'd be interested in that, wouldn't you?

EDISON: Careful, Henry; you sound like a politician already.

HARDING (*offstage*): Hello!

FORD: It's good business. That's all it is. Maybe we can't fix this country. But we sure as hell can crank her up and aim her down the right road.

(*Harding rushes back in*)

HARDING: Something's out there. Something big.

FORD: An animal?

HARDING: I hope it's an animal.

FORD: What do you mean?

HARDING: If it's not an animal, it's a man, and he's not answering me.

FORD (*pause; steps forward*): HELLO! Is somebody there? (*Pause*) Nobody's there—(*Sound can be heard*)

HARDING: Did you hear that?

FORD: Why would anybody be hiding from us?

HARDING: Do you know how many death threats I get in the mail every day?

FORD (*dismissing him*): So do I—

HARDING: I get dozens!

FORD: I get hundreds of them! (*Edison can't believe their petulance*)

HARDING: This trip has been front-page news. The whole country knows we're up here.

(*Sound heard again*)

EDISON: Even I heard that.

FORD (*louder than previously*): You see this gun? I've had it forever; wouldn't walk out the door without it.

79

HARDING: It's a beauty.

FORD: Get behind the trees. (*Ford hands Harding the tire iron. He picks up a branch and hands one to Edison, whispers*) Take this—

EDISON (*whispering*): I will not!

FORD: Take it! There could be more than one of 'em!

EDISON (*won't take it*): You want me to yell "Bang-Bang," too?

HARDING: I see something—

FORD: Where?

HARDING: Back behind the deer. The bushes moved.

(*Sound of a low growl*)

EDISON: That's not the deer.

FORD: Look!

(*Edison steps out from behind the tree*)

EDISON: It's a wolf! Two of them!

FORD: They're after the deer.

EDISON: No, Henry; they want your carrots.

FORD: The deer's scared. I bet the wolves smelled it.

(*Harding, who's been quietly watching, suddenly lets loose with a wolf cry and runs offstage toward the deer*)

HARDING (*offstage*): CLEAR OUT! YOU HEAR ME! (*Another wolf cry*)

FORD: Geez Louise!

HARDING (*offstage*): AND DON'T COME BACK! (*Howl*)

EDISON (*to Ford*): Where was that sanitarium, you remember? (*Howl. Harding returns, pleased with himself*)

HARDING: You see them tuck tail and run?

FORD: What did you do that for?

HARDING: They would have gobbled him down right in front of us.

FORD: So let them! That's nature's way; the deer's dinner, sooner or later; why get in their way?

HARDING: That deer has survived your car and your carrots and he's still here! And when we get found, I'll

81

send a vet back and, by God, that deer will outlive this day the same as we do! (*Howl*) Did you *see* them go!

FORD: Calm yourself, Harding.

HARDING: I had to listen to your birdcalls, didn't I? (*Howl*)

FORD: You want somebody to hear you?

HARDING: Yes!! (*Howl*)

FORD: Stop it! Stop it! Call for help like a human being!

(*Harding howls again*)

EDISON: I don't know which is worse; the Bird Man or the Wolf Boy.

HARDING: I feel like I'm fifteen! Why don't we put your phonograph on again?

EDISON: No!

HARDING (*to Ford*): Do the Ripple? A do-si-do?

FORD: You're demented, you know that? You're some kind of lunatic!

HARDING: It's a celebration, Henry. Don't be a party pooper.

FORD: Damn it all; show a little restraint, you're a grown man! Act your age! Mr. Edison—

EDISON: If I acted my age, you'd toss dirt on me.

(*Harding laughs, even Edison smiles*)

FORD: Now let's settle down here. (*They do*) Alright then. We should take turns calling for help.

HARDING: Go to it.

FORD (*rising, bellows*): HELP! (*Pleased with himself, turns to Harding*) Next.

HARDING: My turn? (*Harding howls*)

FORD: Mr. Edison?

(*Edison, sitting, rises; goes over to the car, pushes horn. Sound of electric car horn. Ford and Harding are excited*)

HARDING: Splendid idea!

FORD: Edison in action!

(*Car horn fades in volume, then out*)

EDISON (*pause*): Help.

FORD (*defensive*): It runs off the battery.

HARDING: You really should have an independent system for the horn and lights. What happens to people when their car gets stranded?

FORD: They sit and yell "help."

EDISON: Maybe when you go to Washington, Henry, Mr. Harding can take over in Detroit.

HARDING: No, thank you.

FORD: It wasn't an offer!

EDISON: What are you going to do, Henry. Run the country during lunch hour?

FORD: That's funny, is it?

EDISON: Maybe you can fill in for George the Fifth and the Pope during coffee breaks.

FORD: And maybe you'll take your head out of a book long enough to see what I'll do!

(*Harding tries to dispel the tension between the men*)

HARDING: I don't know what I'll do when I retire.

(They turn on Harding)

EDISON: Buy a house with a big backyard. You can handshake the whole neighborhood.

HARDING: I just sold my old newspaper, the *Marion Star*. Maybe in a few years when the general public won't want to lynch me on sight, I can go back into the newspaper business. *(To Ford)* Be nice to blast somebody else on the front page.

EDISON: I published my own paper when I was fifteen. Printed it in the boxcar of a train I worked on. We had a picture of a steam engine on the front page and our credo underneath: "Reason, Justice and Equality never had enough weight on earth to govern the councils of men."

FORD: Who said that?

EDISON: I did.

FORD *(to Harding)*: What was your motto?

HARDING: "All The News in Caledonia." It wasn't much of a motto.

FORD: You want words to live by, give me Emerson anytime. "Every man is a government within himself." From "Self-Reliance." Have you read it?

HARDING: No.

FORD: Read it. You should. "To be great is to be misunderstood." "Beware when God lets loose a thinker on this planet. Then all things are at risk."

EDISON: A great thinker thinks. That doesn't mean he changes anything.

FORD: That's not so—

EDISON: Name me one great thinker who has changed the world, and changed it for the better.

HARDING (*thinking*): Well . . .

FORD: He asked me, not you. Jesus Christ. . . . what about him?

EDISON: I've got nothing against the man. I like a good rabble rouser. And he said some very pretty things, all suitable for embroidery. But did he improve the world?

FORD: Of course he did!

EDISON: Did he say or do one thing to make the human race less foolish? Make us wiser, or even less hateful to each other? Did he leave behind anything except new slogans we can use to kill our neighbors?

HARDING: You did, though. You both did. You've improved our world.

EDISON: We've made things easier, I won't argue that. We live faster lives. But what's better?

FORD: What are you talking about?

EDISON: We're toymakers, Henry. That's all we are.

FORD: If you want to spit in your own soup, fine, but leave mine alone. I've made the world a better place, and I'm proud of it.

EDISON: Oh yes. We can hop in your Model Ts after working all day and drive home to our families who we can stare at all night, thanks to my light bulb. Or we can all hop back into our cars and drive to our moviehouse where we won't have to talk at all. And when somebody finally steals even more of my patents and makes projectors cheap enough for every home, we won't even need to get out of our easy chairs to ignore each other. Where's your "better" world, Henry?

FORD: Every kind of knowledge benefits mankind.

EDISON: Don't get noble on me, Henry. Nobody cares about mankind, not even you. We're not devised to comprehend the notion; we've got the survival skill of selfishness built into our core.

FORD: Not mine.

EDISON: No? You want to save this country because *you* want the gratification of that dubious achievement. You want to benefit mankind, but I've never heard you say one kind word to your own son since I've known you. I'm no better! I gave up on my own children as soon as I realized they weren't me, and even worse, they didn't wish they were.

FORD (*seething*): Edsel loves the car business.

EDISON: Edsel loves you and what's that gotten him? A bleeding ulcer and shoes he'll never fill, because whenever he tries to, you slip them back on! Henry, it makes me want to scream when I hear people talk about loving "humanity." It's such a bald-faced excuse to climb over everybody's back so the crowd can get a better look at you.

HARDING: I think you're right.

FORD: Well isn't that nice; Mister Five-Time-Mentally-Broken-to-Pieces thinks you're right. You know what I think, Edison? I think you think too much!

EDISON: And I think most folks will go to any extreme not to think at all.

(*Ford walks away from Edison*)

HARDING: I tried to surround myself with thinkers. Specialists on every subject: fuel, finance, war; I collected them all. I'd listen to one expert tell me the solution was obvious: I should see things his way or the world would end before lunch. I'd agree, then meet with the second expert who'd tell me the exact opposite, and expert three would tell me to fire the first two. It makes your head spin! And they call this "political science." Give me cigars and backrooms; at least we got things done that way.

EDISON: You know what got the Nobel Prize for Science this year? Something called the "photoelectric effect." A paper written by a twenty-six-year old I've read three times and still don't have a clue what he's talking about. These kids like Einstein are off in the clouds somewhere! Thoughts conceived for their own sake! Nothing we can build or touch; thoughts for the cerebral recreation of our great thinkers while the rest of us go to hell in a handbasket. Welcome to the Modern Age.

(*Ford approaches them*)

FORD: What a couple of crybabies. That's right! Two big crybabies! Boo hoo hoo, the world's too tough; whining like a couple of sob sisters. You don't know how lucky you are!

EDISON: I'm sure you'll tell us, Henry.

FORD: DON'T LAUGH AT ME! (*To Harding*) You got handed the opportunity of a lifetime and you—(*To Edison*) have more brains than you know what to do with. And what do you do? Throw your hands up! Scratch your head and watch the world mow you down, like that damn deer, while you sit here sniveling about the Modern Age. Goddamn it, face the facts, we made it! We *are* the Modern Age!

VOICE (*offstage*): Mr. Ford?

(*Ford, hearing the voice from the woods jumps back, startled. Harding and Edison rise as Secret Service man Col. Edmund Starling enters. Starling is a lean, exacting Secret Service man. Starched, mustached and perfectly groomed*)

HARDING: Colonel!

COL. STARLING: Mr. President!

HARDING: Thank God you found us.

COL. STARLING (*to Harding*): Are you alright, sir?

FORD: Did you have to sneak up on us like that? Where's your car?

COL. STARLING: I'm on foot, sir. Somebody cut the wires on my battery.

(*Starling looks from Ford to Edison*)

FORD: Did they?

COL. STARLING: Yes sir.

FORD: Couldn't you just borrow another car?

COL. STARLING: I did just that, Mr. Ford. And I followed your tracks until a few minutes ago—

FORD: And . . . ?

COL. STARLING: I ran out of fuel, sir.

FORD: Well, that's no problem. We've got plenty of that.

(*The Colonel spots the crashed car*)

COL. STARLING: You're lucky to be alive. What happened?

FORD: A deer ran us off the road!

COL. STARLING: A deer?

FORD: Forget it; let's siphon some gasoline and get on our way.

COL. STARLING: Before we do that, gentlemen, I think it's my obligation to point out that this prank of yours could have had tragic consequences. You've endangered the President and the entire country.

EDISON: Tell you what, son. When we get back to camp we'll all stand in the corner. But let's get there first.

COL. STARLING (*to Harding*): I am pleased to report, though, sir, that no one knows you're gone. Except for Mr. Ford's wife and son.

FORD (*pleased*): He was looking for me, was he? He got worried, Edsel?

COL. STARLING: No, sir. I borrowed his car, so I had to tell him.

FORD (*annoyed*): Fine. Let's get to work. (*Goes toward his car*) I know I have a siphon back here somewhere.

COL. STARLING: Mr. President—(*moves Harding away from the men*) Washington has been trying to raise you in the radio car. I told our operator you were sleeping and didn't want to be disturbed, but they won't be put off.

HARDING: Is it urgent?

COL. STARLING: It's your wife. I think you should call Mrs. Harding as soon as you're back in camp.

HARDING (*troubled*): Well, Colonel, maybe in the morning.

COL. STARLING: I strongly recommend you speak with her tonight, sir. You know how persistent she is.

EDISON (*to Starling*): I think the man can decide if he wants to talk to his own wife.

(*Col. Starling looks over at Edison*)

COL. STARLING: I see your hearing has improved, Mr. Edison.

EDISON: And I see your manners haven't, Colonel.

HARDING: Come on now, boys! We're almost home free; let's keep things friendly.

(*Starling has stepped over to the fire, picks up the can of carrots*)

COL. STARLING: What are these orange . . . lumps?

(*Ford steps back in view*)

FORD: Carrots. Look here, Starling; you put the tube down the gas tank. You should be able to siphon at least a gallon or two. All you need to do is suck at the tube and get a vacuum. Go to it.

93

(*Starling is not pleased*)

COL. STARLING: Mr. Ford, I take my orders from the President.

(*Edison and Ford stare at Harding*)

HARDING (*backing down*): Do as Mr. Ford says, please.

COL. STARLING: Sir.

FORD: Start sucking, Colonel. (*Starling goes to hose Ford is holding for him*)

(*Harding looks up at the sky, takes a deep breath*)

HARDING: A full moon.

EDISON: Of course.

HARDING: Just look at it.

FORD (*watching Starling put the siphon in his mouth*): I'd rather watch this.

(*Harding and Edison look at the moon*)

HARDING: Have you read any of Jules Verne's books, Mr. Edison?

EDISON: With great pleasure.

HARDING: What wonderful fantasies.

EDISON: Fantasies? I don't think so. It's just his builders aren't born yet. A fantasy's something that can never be.

HARDING: I had always wanted to be Phineas Fogg or Captain Nemo. Or the Best-loved President.

(*Starling starts coughing, spitting; the vacuum has worked*)

FORD: We've got gas. (*To Starling*) You want something to take that taste out of your mouth?

COL. STARLING: Yes—

FORD: Try some carrots.

(*Starling turns away from Ford*)

HARDING: How far away is the car, Colonel?

COL. STARLING: Half a mile, not much more. We can walk it.

EDISON (*sitting*): You can.

HARDING: Why don't you collect the car and come back for us?

95

COL. STARLING: Sir, if I could have a word? (*Starling draws Harding aside, annoyed*) Mr. President, you are my responsibility. I will come back for the others, but I would like you to come with me. It's my job to see nothing happens to you.

HARDING: Then you're already too late, Colonel.

(*Ford and Edison are now watching*)

COL. STARLING: I insist, sir. You must come with me.

HARDING: Who is in charge here, Colonel?

COL. STARLING: Considering your actions tonight, sir, I'd say that's debatable.

HARDING: You get that car or I'll kick your ass back to Washington. And that's not debatable.

COL. STARLING: Sir. (*Exits, holding gas can and siphon*)

EDISON: Now that's an executive decision.

FORD: That boy's going to be out mulching the Rose Garden.

HARDING: Gosh, they're obnoxious. Like an army of mothers. With guns.

FORD: I'll clean house of the whole bunch of them. Hire a private security force.

HARDING: You should. You should. (*Pause*) When will you make your announcement?

FORD: Well, I could do it tonight or tomorrow morning.

HARDING: I'd like to radio Washington tonight. They should get some advance warning that I'll be resigning. Especially poor Coolidge. Give him time to start abbreviating the oath of office.

FORD: Don't you worry about Coolidge. He won't be there long.

HARDING (*defensively*): Two more years.

FORD: Gives me plenty of time. I'll be the first President in history to campaign with a fully designed four-year plan. Where we're going, how we'll get there and who's coming for the ride. I hope that will include you, Mr. Edison. We're going to light some fires, we are. We're going to watch bureaucrats pop like popcorn. We'll take the bloat out of this government and boil it down to size. People will like that, you wait and see. And what they'll like even more are lower taxes and money back in their pockets. That's right. We'll give them a country they can afford for once. Get our hands back on our own treasury. So the first thing we've got to do is get rid of the Jews.

HARDING (*pause*): Excuse me?

FORD: Come on now, Harding. Don't get coy with me. You don't owe them anymore, and you know what I'm talking about.

HARDING: I don't.

FORD: You never read the "Protocols of Zion"?

HARDING: No—

FORD: It's their whole plan, spelled out in black and white. How the Jews and the Masons will bring the Christian world to its knees, all schemed out a thousand years ago.

EDISON: The document's a forgery; there's never been any proof it's real.

FORD: It's proven itself! Open your eyes! Who squeezed a profit from the blood of our boys fighting the Kaiser? Who's taken over our newspapers? Who tells us what to wear and watch and listen to? Who's out there in Hollywood right now, trying to turn California into the Promised Land? A goddamn gaggle of international Jews, that's who! The invisible government! A whole race that makes their money on the rest of us breaking our backs! You bet it's true! I don't think I've ever seen a Jew do a real day's work.

EDISON: I have. I work with Jews in my lab. They work as hard as the rest of us.

FORD: With their heads, maybe. Figuring how to steal your ideas and your whole operation. (*To Harding*) Have you ever seen one work with his hands? I'll pay anybody a thousand dollars to show me a Jew farmer, dead or alive!

HARDING: You can't be serious!

FORD: You bet I am! We start with the Jews. Take them down a notch, that's the solution. And the rest of their kind will sink back into the mud with them; the munitions makers, the union boys. Put the newspapers back into the hands of some patriots for a change! And think about the children! They're our future! We've got to see to it they're brought up in the right kind of homes. And schools! We'll jump right on them. Teach them how to teach something worth learning. Rewrite the bunk in these schoolbooks and tell our kids the truth about this world!

EDISON: Which is what, Henry? You want to teach them to hate as well as you do?

FORD: Me? What about you? Who stole your movie pictures, who stole your life's work out from under your

99

nose! You hate the Jews as much as I do! You've got to!

EDISON: Not so much as I hate the English, who picked my pocket more politely or the French, to whom lying is a national sport. Or the Spaniards or Italians —And even more than human beings, I hate politicians; the echoes of whatever empty crowd they're trying to impress that day. I hate everybody! Which is why I shouldn't be President. And why you shouldn't be, either. A country's not a car, Henry, you can't handpick your parts—

FORD: Don't tell me what I can do! Don't you dare. You sound like my father! If I listened to him, I would have been riding a tractor all my life. I know what I can do! I've done it! (*Points to Harding*) And what has he done? You didn't vote for him, *he* didn't even vote for himself! The man doesn't have a thought in his head—

EDISON: He's smart enough to know he can't do the job. And he hates himself for it. But that's better than blaming a whole race of people for no other reason than your own ignorance.

FORD: So I'm stupid, now. Is that it?

HARDING: Alright now; this has gone far enough—

FORD: Stay out of this! (*To Edison*) You think I'm a rube, don't you? A clodhopper who got lucky?

EDISON: I didn't say that—

FORD: Well, I'm glad I'm not the "genius" you are. Because I know what people want. I gave it to them once, and I'll give it to them again and when I do, watch out, it'll be another American Revolution. So don't you dare look down on me like you're my father or my judge or some know-it-all Jew. This country needs me! And I'm not going to stand here like some genius and think about it while I watch it drowned!

EDISON: You scare me, Henry.

(*Sound of the car in the distance*)

HARDING: That's the Colonel.

FORD: It's about time.

EDISON: You can't. You can't be President. I can't let that happen.

FORD: There's nothing you can do to stop me.

EDISON: There is, if I have to.

(*Ford stares at Edison, who doesn't back down*)

HARDING (*pause*): I don't understand.

EDISON: Do you really think all this hate talk of yours will look pretty in the headlines?

FORD: It might not look pretty, but it will get me elected. There's plenty of people out there who think just like I do.

EDISON: Maybe there are. I don't want to find out. But Henry, if you make one move to announce your candidacy, I'll make an announcement of my own. And I can promise you that once you've given Harding the heave-ho for moral degeneracy, the country won't be in the mood for yours.

(*Sound of car getting closer*)

FORD (*furious and hurt*): You son of a bitch. Anything I ever said to you was private conversation. Private!

EDISON: Then don't make me say more.

FORD: Nobody will believe you! Not over me! Some half-deaf dinosaur who can't remember his own name half the time—

EDISON: "Agnes." Was that her name? The servant girl you sent back to Finland. Or was that the other one? The stenographer you gave the car to and the boat and the farm. "Evangeline." Wasn't that her name? Or was that the baby?

(*Sound of car stopping*)

COL. STARLING (*offstage*): Men!

EDISON: I don't want to remember, Henry. But I will.

HARDING: Mr. Edison, Henry; we all need to do some thinking . . .

(*Starling appears, annoyed*)

COL. STARLING: Sir!

HARDING: Wait in the car, Colonel.

COL. STARLING: Sir, it's almost—

HARDING: *Wait in the car!* (*Starling exits*) Henry, listen to me. Henry! I see two separate issues here. Two different decisions. Now what you decide to do about yourself, that's your business. But what about my situation? You're still going to the press, you're still going to tell them—

FORD: Tell them yourself! Can't you even do that much? Stand up for yourself for once in your life!

(*Sound of gunshot. Starling enters*)

103

HARDING: You shot the deer?

COL. STARLING: Of course I did—

HARDING: Why did you do that? WHY DID YOU HAVE TO DO THAT?

COL. STARLING: He was lame, wasn't he? What else did you expect me to do? I put the animal out of its pain. (*Harding turns away*) Sir? You couldn't have brought him back with you. You want to explain to the press corps how you hit him? I can get you all back to your tents tonight with no one seeing you. I'll come back for your car myself. And tomorrow morning, it will be business as usual. (*Pause*) Is that acceptable? Mr. President? (*Harding says nothing*) Mr. Ford, Mr. Edison; I expect we can keep this little adventure to ourselves?

EDISON: You can expect to keep your job, Colonel.

(*Starling looks at his watch*)

COL. STARLING: Mr. President, you really haven't been gone all that long. If you call Mrs. Harding right now, I don't think anything will seem amiss. Can we go, sir?

(*Harding and Starling exit*)

FORD: That's what you want for your President?

EDISON: The Starlings run the government. Not him. He'll keep shaking hands on the lawn, as long as he doesn't get in the way.

FORD: It's wrong.

EDISON: It's democracy. And as long as we've got one, we won't get the best or the worst. Just something in the middle.

FORD: Mr. Edison? How could you do this to me?

EDISON: He couldn't stand to see the deer killed. He tried to stop you. I didn't. And you wouldn't have blinked. There's something in him we don't have.

FORD: Weakness.

EDISON: Maybe so. But maybe I hope somebody like him will be there to take pity on the rest of us dumb animals when we need it.

FORD: I want to be a great man. What's wrong with that?

EDISON: You're a great businessman. A great manufacturer. You'll be remembered as the man who yanked this country into another age, whether they wanted to go or not. But you're not a leader, Henry. A leader's got to know where he's going. And he's got to have somebody behind him when he gets there.

(*Edison puts a hand on Ford's shoulder*) Come on now. I keep waiting for this vacation to start.

(*Starling enters*)

COL. STARLING: Boys! We're leaving! With or without you! (*Starling exits, they glare after him*)

EDISON: I really hate to follow that fellow, but I'm hungry. (*Ford doesn't respond. Edison sees how disturbed he is*) You know what, Henry? I am working on that machine to contact the dead. I want to prove you wrong about reincarnation.

FORD: What if I'm right?

EDISON: Then I'll probably come back as a deer. And you'll be back as a tire. (*They start to go; Edison stops*) Billy.

FORD: What?

EDISON: Billy Eagan. That's his name. My friend who drowned.

(*Harding enters*)

HARDING: Gentlemen. I wanted to let you know I won't be here tomorrow morning. I'll be leaving early. (*Sound of car horn*) They need me in Massachusetts to dedicate Plymouth Rock. They moved it.

FORD: Why would they move Plymouth Rock?

HARDING: Well, it was never all that close to the water. And it's high. The only way any Pilgrims could have really landed on it is if they were dropped by balloon. This way all the people who come to see it will be happier.

FORD: Aw shit!

(*Ford exits. Harding looks at Edison, who gestures for Harding to go ahead of him*)

EDISON: Mr. President.

(*Edison and Harding exit. Slow blackout. End of play.*)